# 30 Minutes
## ... To Write a
## Marketing Plan

**John Westwood**

KOGAN
PAGE

## YOURS TO HAVE AND TO HOLD
### BUT NOT TO COPY

The publication you are reading is protected by copyright law. This means that the publisher could take you and your employer to court and claim heavy legal damages if you make unauthorised photocopies from these pages. Photocopying copyright material without permission is no different from stealing a magazine from a newsagent, only it doesn't seem like theft.

The Copyright Licensing Agency (CLA) is an organisation which issues licences to bring photocopying within the law. It has designed licensing services to cover all kinds of special needs in business, education and government.

If you take photocopies from books, magazines and periodicals at work your employer should be licensed with the CLA. Make sure you are protected by a photocopying licence.

The Copyright Licensing Agency Limited, 90 Tottenham Court Road, London, W1P 0LP. Tel: 0171 436 5931. Fax: 0171 436 3986.

First published in 1997
Reprinted 1997

Apart from any fair dealing for the purposes of research or private study, or criticism or review, as permitted under the Copyright, Designs and Patents Act 1988, this publication may only be reproduced, stored or transmitted, in any form or by any means, with the prior permission in writing of the publishers, or in the case of reprographic reproduction in accordance with the terms and licences issued by the CLA. Enquiries concerning reproduction outside those terms should be sent to the publishers at the undermentioned address:

Kogan Page Limited
120 Pentonville Road
London N1 9JN

© John Westwood, 1997

The right of John Westwood to be identified as author of this work has been asserted by him in accordance with the Copyright, Designs and Patents Act 1988.

**British Library Cataloguing in Publication Data**

A CIP record for this book is available from the British Library.

ISBN 0 7494 2363 3

Typeset by Saxon Graphics Ltd, Derby
Printed in England by Clays Ltd, St Ives plc

# CONTENTS

## The 30 Minutes Series

*The Kogan Page 30 Minutes Series* has been devised to give your confidence a boost when faced with tackling a new skill or challenge for the first time.

So the next time you're thrown in at the deep end and want to bring your skills up to scratch or pep up your career prospects, turn to the *30 Minutes Series* for help!

*Titles available are:*

30 Minutes Before Your Job Interview
30 Minutes Before a Meeting
30 Minutes Before a Presentation
30 Minutes to Boost Your Communication Skills
30 Minutes to Succeed in Business Writing
30 Minutes to Master the Internet
30 Minutes to Make the Right Decision
30 Minutes to Prepare a Job Application
30 Minutes to Write a Business Plan
30 Minutes to Write a Marketing Plan
30 Minutes to Write a Report
30 Minutes to Write Sales Letters

*Available from all good booksellers.*
*For further information on the series, please contact:*

Kogan Page, 120 Pentonville Road, London N1 9JN
Tel: 0171 278 0433 Fax: 0171 837 6348

**1**

# WHAT IS MARKETING PLANNING?

A company's management has many important roles. It sets objectives, and develops plans, policies, procedures, strategies and tactics. It organises and co-ordinates, directs and controls, motivates and communicates. Planning is only one of its roles but a vital one: the company's corporate or business plan guides it forward.

The marketing plan is an important part of this overall plan. The marketing planning process therefore needs to be carried out as part of the company planning and budgeting process.

The marketing plan sets out the marketing objectives of the company and suggests strategies for achieving them. It does not include all the company's objectives and strategies. There will also be production, financial and personnel objectives, none of which can be set in isolation. The plan for the company comprises a number of sub-plans *including* the overall company marketing plan which need to be agreed and co-ordinated into one overall business plan.

In turn, the marketing plan can be broken down into a number of smaller marketing plans for individual products or areas, which can be prepared as and when needed.

This practical book includes only as much theory as is necessary to understand the planning process. As you make your way through, you will be shown the principles of marketing planning in a way that will make it easy for you to put together any type of marketing plan.

Increasingly, sales and marketing personnel are having to put together individual plans for a product or area very quickly. This book is designed with this in mind. You will find that adopting and following the formal structure of the plan (shown later) will make it easier for you to order your thoughts and the facts logically. It will be easier for:

■ people to follow your arguments and to see how you reached your conclusions

■ you to present a professional-looking and complete document, even from a relatively small amount of information.

## What is selling?

Selling is a straightforward concept which involves persuading a customer to buy a product. It brings in 'today's orders'. However, it is only one aspect of the marketing process.

## What is marketing?

The dictionary definition of marketing is: 'the provision of goods or services to meet consumers' needs'. In other words, marketing involves finding out what the customer wants, matching a company's products to meet those requirements and, in the process making a profit for the company. Successful marketing means having the right product available in the right place at the right time and making sure that the customer is aware of it. Unlike selling, it aims to bring in 'tomorrow's orders'.

Bringing together the abilities of the company and the requirements of the customer occurs in the 'real world'; the 'marketing environment', which is not controlled by individuals or companies, is constantly changing and must be monitored continuously. Marketing therefore means considering:

- The abilities of the company
- The requirements of the customer
- The marketing environment.

The abilities of the company can be managed by its marketing department. They can control the four main elements of a company's operation, often called 'the marketing mix'. The marketing mix, or the four Ps relate to:

- The product sold (Product)
- The pricing policy (Price)
- How the product is promoted (Promotion)
- Methods of distribution (Place)

These are four controllable variables which allow a company to come up with a policy which is profitable and satisfies its customers.

## What is marketing planning?

The term marketing planning is used to describe the methods of applying marketing resources to achieve marketing objectives. It is used to segment markets, identify market

7

position, forecast market size, and plan viable market share within each market segment. The marketing planning process involves:

- Carrying out marketing research within and outside the company
- Looking at the company's strengths and weaknesses
- Making assumptions
- Forecasting
- Setting marketing objectives
- Generating marketing strategies
- Defining programmes
- Setting budgets
- Reviewing the results and revising the objectives, strategies or programmes.

Marketing planning will:

- Make better use of company resources to identify marketing opportunities
- Encourage team spirit and company identity
- Help the company to move towards achieving its goals.

Marketing planning is a continuous process, so the plan will need to be reviewed and updated as it is implemented.

## Stages in the preparation of a marketing plan

The stages in the preparation of a marketing plan are shown in Figure 1.1.

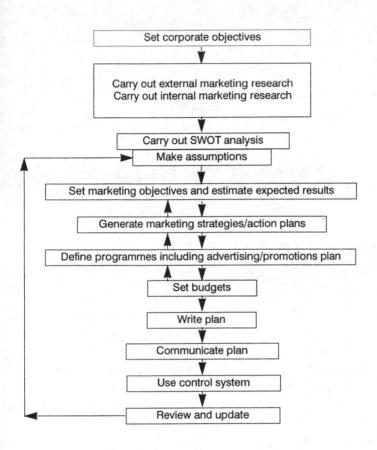

**Figure 1.1** *The marketing planning process*

# 2

# SITUATION ANALYSIS

Before you can decide on your marketing objectives and future strategies, you need to understand the position of your company and its products in the marketplace. Situation analysis can help you do this:

- It reviews the economic and business climate
- It considers where the company stands in its strategic markets and key sales areas
- It looks at the strengths and weaknesses of the company – its organisation, its performance and its key products
- It compares the company with its competitors
- It identifies opportunities and threats.

Before you can start this process, you need to carry out a marketing audit.

## The marketing audit

The marketing audit is a detailed examination of the

company's marketing environment, specific marketing activities and internal marketing system. It examines the company's markets, customers and competitors in the context of the overall economic and political environment. It involves carrying out marketing research and collecting historical data about your company and its products. It is an iterative process. Only when you start to analyse your own in-house data do you realise which external market sectors you need to look at, and once you look at the external data you may notice applications that are small for your company, but larger in a market context and therefore require further investigation.

## The marketing environment – market research

At the same time as considering historical sales data for your company, you need to collect information that will allow it to be put into perspective. This involves market research – collecting information about your markets and then analysing it in the context of the marketing of the products.

In its simplest form, market research can be defined as a combination of in-house experience, sales force market intelligence and marketing research. From these sources, we extract marketing information which allows us to analyse, compare and evaluate. Market research is used to:

- Give a description of the market
- Monitor how the market changes
- Decide on actions to be taken and evaluate the results.

Market research data consists of *primary* and *secondary* data.

*Primary data* comes from primary sources, ie from the marketplace and is obtained either by carrying out field research directly or by commissioning a consultant or market research company to do it for you.

11

*Secondary data* is not obtained directly from fieldwork, and market research based on secondary data sources is referred to as desk research. Desk research involves the collection of data from existing sources, such as:

- Government statistics (from the Central Statistical Office)
- Company information (from Companies House or directories such as Kompass or Kelly's)
- Trade directories
- Trade associations
- Ready-made reports (from companies such as Keynote, Euromonitor, Mintel, and Frost & Sullivan)

The market research information for your marketing plan will consist of *market information* and *product information*.

*Market information* needs to cover:

| | |
|---|---|
| ■ The market's size | How big is it?<br>How is it segmented/structured? |
| ■ Its characteristics | Who are the main customers?<br>Who are the main suppliers?<br>What are the main products sold? |
| ■ The state of the market | Is it a new market?<br>A mature market?<br>A saturated market? |
| ■ How well are companies doing? | Related to the market as a whole?<br>In relation to each other? |
| ■ Channels of distribution | What are they? |
| ■ Methods of communication | What methods are used – press, TV, direct mail?<br>What types of sales promotion? |
| ■ Financial | Are there problems caused by taxes or duties?<br>Import restrictions? |

- Legal
  - Patent situation
  - Product standards
  - Legislation relating to agents
  - Trademarks/copyright
  - Protection of intellectual property (designs/software, etc)

- Developments
  - What new areas of the market are developing?
  - What new products are developing?
  - Is new legislation or regulation likely?

*Product information* relates to your own company, your competitors and the customers:

- Potential customers
  - Who are they?
  - Where are they located?
  - Who are the market leaders in their fields?

- Your own company
  - Do existing products meet customers' needs?
  - Is product development necessary?
  - Are completely new products required?
  - What would be the potential of a new product?
  - How is your company perceived in the market?

- Your competitors
  - Who are they?
  - How do they compare with your company in size?
  - Where are they located?
  - Are they owned by key potential customers?

> Do they operate in the same market sectors as you?
>
> What products do they manufacture/sell?
>
> How does their pricing compare with your own?
>
> What sales/distribution channels do they use?
>
> Have they recently introduced new products?

The first step towards finding this information is to contact the relevant trade association, which could give details of companies in the same field. There may also be trade publications and statistics. The trade association may also have copies of published reports which could be viewed at their offices rather than buying them. You may also be able to get relevant statistics from the Central Statistical Office and obtain UK competitors' annual accounts from Companies House.

Figure 2.1 shows the type of information that a company could produce, using information from these sources together with its knowledge of its own sales.

## Internal market research

As well as external market research, your company has a wealth of data that is invaluable in the preparation of a marketing plan. There is likely to be so much data that you cannot easily see which information is the most important. Often data is not available in the right form. You may have overall sales data, but not data itemised for individual product lines or market segments.

The relevant historical data is basically sales/order data separated and analysed in such a way that it reflects the key market segments into which you sell your products.

| UK market share – ball valves | | |
|---|---|---|
| Company | £ | % |
| Equipment MFG Co. | 1,000 | 10 |
| Biggs Valves | 2,200 | 22 |
| Sparco Valves | 800 | 8 |
| DVK (German) | 1,600 | 16 |
| Texas Valves (USA) | 800 | 8 |
| Others | 3,600 | 36 |
| Total | 10,000 | 100 |

**Figure 2.1:** *Market share information*

# What is market segmentation ?

Different customers have different needs. They do not all require the same product or product benefits, and not all customers will buy a particular product for the same reasons. Market segmentation allows you to consider the markets you are actually in and the markets you should be in. It is useful to split your customer base up into groups of customers who all have similar needs. Each of these groups constitutes a market segment.

For consumer goods and services, it is usual to define market segments by using methods of classification which separate consumers by socio-economic group, age, sex, occupation or region.

The marketing of industrial goods and services is different, because the customer is usually another company or a government department. The number of customers is likely to be closer to 10,000 than 10 million and may only be a few hundred in the case of suppliers to power stations, coal mines, etc. The main ways of defining market segments here are:

- By geographical area

15

- By industry or industry sub-sector
- By product
- By application
- By size of end-user
- By distribution channel – distributor, equipment manufacturer, end-user.

Segmentation can also be based on:

- Order size
- Order frequency
- Type of decision-maker.

The key is to let the marketplace segment itself, because the individual segments exist independently of the company and its products.

## Information checklist

It is useful to prepare an information checklist for a marketing plan before you start to collect data. The exact detail will vary depending on the scope of your plan, but it should include details of the segmentation that you want for sales, the split of your customer base and competitor activity/market shares.

### Information required:

*1. Sales history*

The last three years' sales by value (including margins where available) for:

- Sales areas/regions
- Product groups
- Main equipment and spares

Also unit sales:

- Numbers of units by model/size

## 2. Customers

Total number of customers by:

- Sales area
- Products bought
- Industry sector, eg food/water/chemicals
- Key customers, ie top 40 by sales turnover

## 3. Competition

- Who are the competitors for each product group?
- What are the market shares for each product for each competitor?

## How to present the figures

Depending on the scope of the plan, the sales data may be split into separate tables geographically, by product, by industry or under all of these categories.

The figures can be easily prepared on computer spreadsheets such as Lotus 1–2–3 or Excel, which allow the data entered into the spreadsheet tables to be displayed graphically as well. It is usual when producing tables of historical data on a spreadsheet to extend the form layout to include columns for the years which the marketing plan will cover. Collect and present information going back two or three full years together with this year's sales. You should show margin information relating to those sales where it is available. You should also adjust figures for inflation and have them available in both their actual and adjusted forms. The columns for future years will remain blank for now as the

17

current task is to record historical and current sales data, but it makes it easier later on to project sales figures so that comparisons can be made and trends can be analysed.

Examples of how the figures could be presented are shown in Figures 2.2 and 2.3.

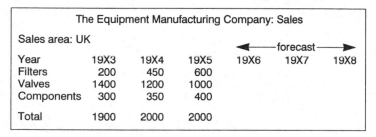

The Equipment Manufacturing Company: Sales

Sales area: UK

| Year | 19X3 | 19X4 | 19X5 | forecast 19X6 | 19X7 | 19X8 |
|------|------|------|------|------|------|------|
| Filters | 200 | 450 | 600 | | | |
| Valves | 1400 | 1200 | 1000 | | | |
| Components | 300 | 350 | 400 | | | |
| Total | 1900 | 2000 | 2000 | | | |

**Figure 2.2:** *Sales figures UK (all products) (all values in £k)*

The Equipment Manufacturing Company: Sales

Sales area: UK
Product: Filters

| Year | 19X3 | 19X4 | 19X5 | forecast 19X6 | 19X7 | 19X8 |
|------|------|------|------|------|------|------|
| Type S | 402 | 396 | 412 | | | |
| Type A | 100 | 120 | 140 | | | |
| Type K | 50 | 100 | 150 | | | |
| Packages | 4 | 8 | 14 | | | |
| Total | 556 | 624 | 716 | | | |

**Figure 2.3:** *Unit sales of filters*

The *profitability* of sales is very important. It is therefore vital also to show the margins being made on the sale of different products. This is shown in Figure 2.4.

This should be broken down to provide more detailed information for each of the main geographical areas.

This information could also be displayed graphically.

| The Equipment Manufacturing Company: Sales | | | | | | |
|---|---|---|---|---|---|---|
| Sales area: UK | | | | | | |
| Year | 19X3 | | 19X4 | | 19X5 | |
| | Sales | Gross Profit | Sales | Gross Profit | Sales | Gross Profit | Comments |
| | £k | % | £k | % | £k | % | |
| Filters | 200 | 40 | 450 | 40 | 600 | 40 | |
| Valves | 1400 | 30 | 1200 | 30 | 1000 | 30 | |
| Components | 300 | 60 | 350 | 60 | 400 | 60 | |
| Total | 1900 | 35.8 | 2000 | 37.5 | 2000 | 39 | |

**Figure 2.4:** *Sales figures (UK) including margin information*

# SWOT analysis

The key process used in situation analysis is SWOT analysis. SWOT stands for:

*'**S**trengths and **W**eaknesses as they relate to our **O**pportunities and **T**hreats in the marketplace.'*

The strengths and weaknesses refer to the company and its products, whereas the opportunities and threats are usually taken to be external factors over which your company has no control. SWOT analysis involves understanding and analysing your strengths and weaknesses and identifying threats to your business as well as opportunities in the marketplace. You can then attempt to exploit your strengths, overcome your weaknesses, grasp your opportunities and defend yourself against threats. SWOT analysis asks the questions that will enable you to decide whether your company and the product will really be able to fulfil your plan and what the constraints will be.

In carrying out SWOT analysis it is usual to list the strengths, weaknesses, opportunities and threats on the same page. This is done by dividing the page into four squares and entering strengths and weaknesses in the top squares and opportunities and threats in the bottom squares.

The number of individual SWOTs will depend on the scope of your plan. First, carry out a SWOT on your company and its organisation. Then do the same for your main competitors and for your products, geographical areas and the market segments covered by your plan. An example of a SWOT analysis is shown in Figure 2.5.

Now we are ready to move on to setting objectives and deciding strategies.

| **Strengths** | **Weaknesses** |
|---|---|
| – Part of large UK group<br>– Good image – quality company<br>– Good resources – financial<br>                – technical<br>– High level of export sales | – Low level of sales in UK<br>– Thought of as 'old fashioned'<br>– Few marketing staff |
| **Opportunities** | **Threats** |
| – Parent company is investing<br>   in new marketing department<br>– New group R & D facility<br>– To develop new products<br>– To open low cost factory in Asia | – Low-priced products from<br>   the Far East<br>– Low-priced products from<br>   the USA |

**Figure 2.5:** *Company SWOT analysis*

# 3

# OBJECTIVES, STRATEGIES AND ACTION PLANS

Having carried out your situation analysis, you are in a position to set your marketing objectives. This is the most important part of preparing a marketing plan.

## What is a marketing objective?

*Objectives are what we want to achieve; strategies are how we get there.*

A marketing objective concerns the balance between products and their markets: it relates to *which products* we want to sell into *which markets*. The means of achieving these objectives, using price, promotion and distribution, are marketing strategies. At the next level down there will be personnel objectives and personnel strategies, advertising objectives and advertising strategies, etc. Further down still there are tactics, action plans and budgets – all to enable us to achieve our objectives. Marketing objectives relate to any of the following:

- Selling existing products into existing markets
- Selling existing products into new markets
- Selling new products into existing markets
- Selling new products into new markets.

Marketing objectives should be definable and quantifiable so that there is an achievable target at which to aim. They should be defined so that, when your marketing plan is implemented, actual performance can be compared with the objective. They should be expressed in terms of values or market shares, and avoid vague terms such as increase, improve or maximise.

The following are examples of marketing objectives:

- To increase sales of the product in the UK by 10 per cent per annum in real terms each year for the next three years
- To increase sales of the product worldwide by 30 per cent in real terms within five years
- To increase market share for the product in the USA from 10 to 15 per cent over two years.

All plans should include marketing objectives for the following:

- Sales turnover for the period of the plan by product and market segment
- Market share for the period of the plan by product and market segment
- Gross profit on sales

## The product portfolio

Since marketing objectives relate to *products* and *markets*, it is important to understand your present position with regard to both before setting the objectives of your marketing plan. The growth and decline of all products follows a life-cycle curve which can be represented as in Figure 3.1.

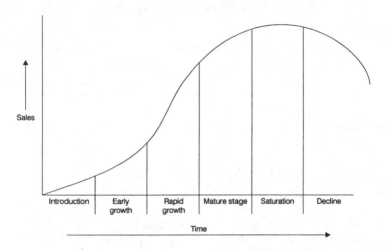

**Figure 3.1:** *Product life-cycle curve*

Ideally, your company will have a portfolio of products all at different stages in their life-cycle, so that balanced growth can be achieved and risks minimised.

## Relative market growth rate and share

In any market the price levels of the major players tend to be broadly similar and in a stable market they will gradually converge. This does not mean that all these companies will make the same level of profit. If one company has a

23

very large market share, it will benefit from economies of scale and will have lower costs and so is likely to have the highest profit margin. It is therefore more able to withstand a price war. Its market share also indicates its ability to generate cash.

> *Market share is very important and your aim should be to achieve market dominance wherever possible.*

*Cash flow* is the most important factor in considering your product portfolio, and your company's ability to generate cash will be dependent to a large extent on the degree of market dominance that you have over your competitors. Some years ago the Boston Consulting Group developed a matrix for classifying a portfolio of products based on relative market shares and relative market growth rates. The Boston Matrix is now widely used by companies in analysing their product portfolio.

The products are colourfully described as:

> **Stars** – high market share/high market growth (cash neutral)
> **Cash cows** – high market share/low market growth (cash generation)
> **Question marks** – low market share/high market growth (cash drain)
> **Dogs** – low market share/low market growth (cash neutral).

Relative market share is the ratio of your market share to the market share of your biggest competitor. This indicates the level of market dominance that you have over your competitors.

Market growth rate is important for two reasons. In a fast-expanding market sales can grow more quickly than in a slow-growing or stable market. In increasing sales, the product will absorb a high level of cash to support increasing advertising, sales coverage, sales support and possibly even investment in additional plant and machinery. For the purposes of marketing planning, high market growth is normally taken as 10 per cent per annum or more.

The products are entered into the quadrants of a matrix as shown in Figure 3.2.

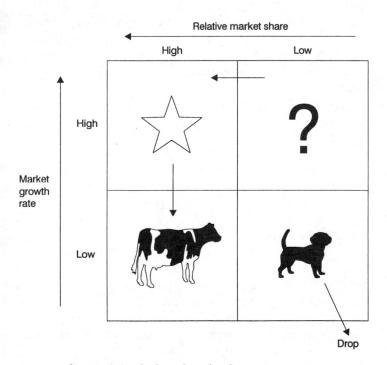

**Figure 3.2:** *Ideal product development sequence*

*Question marks* can be either newly-launched products which have not yet fulfilled expectation, or products that are declining and need further evaluation as to their long-term viability.

*Dogs* have low market share and are generally unprofitable. These products are the ones you should consider dropping from the product portfolio.

*Stars* incur high marketing, research and development costs, but also contribute considerably to profits. They are, broadly speaking, neutral from the point of view of cash generation.

*Cash cows* are mature products with a high market share but low market growth. They generate high profits and require only a small amount of marketing investment and no research and development spending to keep them where they are.

Figure 3.3 shows an example of a product portfolio matrix.

The Type S filters and ball valves are both *cash cows*, but ball valves are declining in both relative market share and becoming less and less profitable. Packages are *question marks*, but will become *stars* if they continue to grow relative market share as the market for them expands. Type A and Type K filters are both moving into the *star* sector, with Type A a little ahead of Type K.

Setting objectives for a marketing plan is not an easy task. Figures for sales turnover or market share cannot just be selected at random. It is an iterative process whereby objectives are set, strategies and action plans are developed and it is then decided whether the planned objectives are impossible, achievable or easy. The objectives are then reappraised and, should they be changed, the strategies and action plans would also need to be re-examined.

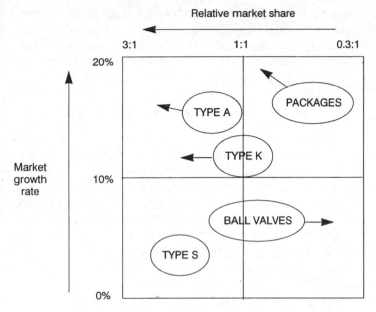

**Figure 3.3:** *Example of a product portfolio matrix*

We can use gap analysis to decide how realistic our objectives are.

## Gap analysis

Gap analysis is a technique with many uses. From the point of view of setting marketing objectives it can be used to help you analyse and close the gap between what your company needs to achieve and what is likely to be achieved if policies are unchanged.

The gap is broken down into its constituent parts. Inflationary growth (price increase) and volume growth. If you are looking for growth of £500,000 a year and know that price increase will contribute £200,000, you will need to have a number of objectives which will generate another £300,000 of volume growth. Your objectives should close the gap and also leave something in reserve, since not all strategies and action plans will bring in the full return that we expect from them.

## What is a marketing strategy?

Marketing strategies are the means by which marketing objectives will be achieved. It is important to understand what strategy is and how it differs from tactics. *Strategies* are the broad methods chosen to achieve specific objectives and describe the means of achieving these objectives within the required time-scale. They do not include the detail of the individual courses of action that will be followed on a day-to-day basis: these are *tactics*.

Marketing strategies relate to general policies for the following:

- Products
  - changing product portfolio/mix
  - dropping, adding or modifying products
  - changing design, quality or performance
  - consolidating/standardising

- Price
  - changing price, terms or conditions for particular product groups in particular market segments
  - skimming policies
  - discount policies

- Promotion
  - changing selling/salesforce organisation
  - changing advertising or sales promotion
  - changing public relations policy
  - increasing/decreasing exhibition coverage

- Distribution
  - changing channels
  - improving service.

There are a number of different types of strategy:

> **Defensive strategies**, designed to prevent loss of existing customers
> **Developing strategies,** designed to offer existing customers a wider range of your products or services
> **Attacking strategies**, designed to generate business through new customers.

A useful way of looking at the types of strategy available is to use a matrix developed by Ansoff, as shown in Figure 3.4.

| | | Low risk | High risk |
|---|---|---|---|
| | | Present product | New product |
| Low risk | Present market | Expand existing market with existing product | Develop new products for existing markets |
| High risk | New market | Sell present product in new markets | Develop or acquire new products to sell into new markets |

**Figure 3.4:** *Ansoff Matrix – the risks of various strategies*

It can be seen from this matrix that the least risky way to try to expand your business is in the areas you know best, ie using your existing products within your existing markets.

## Pricing strategies

Of the many types of pricing strategies and tactics that can be considered, most can be broadly classified as either skimming or penetration policies.

29

*Skimming* – This involves entering the market at a high price level and 'skimming' off as much profit as possible. As competition enters the market, the price level would be adjusted as necessary.

*Penetration.* The opposite of skimming: a company deliberately sets the price low. A penetration policy encourages more customers to purchase the product, which increases the company's sales turnover and also its market share.

## Action plans

Once you have selected the outline strategies and tactics to achieve your marketing objectives, you need to turn these strategies into programmes or action plans that will enable you to give clear instructions to your staff. Each action plan should include:

- Current position – where you are now
- Aims – what to do/where do you want to go?
- Action – what you need to do to get there
- Person responsible – who will do it?
- Start date
- Finish date
- Budgeted cost

Each action plan needs to be broken down into its component parts. Figure 3.5 shows an example of an action plan designed for the strategy of 'carry out a mail shot'.

Each action could be broken down into a number of parts. For example, in the preparation of the brochure there would be a number of stages, including:

- Having photographs taken
- Preparation of technical information by engineering department
- Preparation of preliminary layout

| Action plan | | | | | | |
|---|---|---|---|---|---|---|
| Department: sales | | | | | | |
| Aim | Current position | Action | By | Start | Finish | Cost |
| Carry out mail shot | Mailing list out of date | Update list | ILH | 1.1.X6 | 1.3.X6 | £200 |
| | No standard letter | Prepare letter | JDT | 1.2.X6 | 1.3.X6 | £25 |
| | No brochure | Prepare new brochure | NBF | 1.11.X5 | 1.3.X6 | £3000 |
| | | Send out | ILH | 1.3.X6 | 1.4.X6 | £500 |

**Figure 3.5:** *Presentation of an action plan*

- Writing copy
- Preparation of artwork
- Final checking
- Printing.

After scheduling your activities on the basis of action plans you should combine the individual action plans and programmes into larger functional programmes (product, pricing, promotion, distribution). These functional programmes would appear in the marketing plan. They would then be developed into an overall schedule – a master programme that could be used for controlling the implementation of the plan. This is the schedule of what/where/how in the written plan. Although only the larger functional programmes and the master programme schedule would appear in the written plan, each of the smaller plans and programmes would need to be communicated to those who have to carry them out.

**4**

# DISTRIBUTION, PROMOTION AND BUDGETS

Promotion means getting the right message to the right people. It involves personal selling, advertising and sales promotion. But first you need to select the right channels for your product and your business from those available. This is part of the distribution plan.

## The distribution plan

The physical distribution of goods is only one aspect of distribution as defined by marketing planners. Distribution involves:

- Marketing channels
- Physical distribution
- Customer service

## Marketing channels

Marketing channels are the means by which a company makes contact with its potential customers. There is a wide variety of different channels that a company can use and Figure 4.1 shows a typical selection.

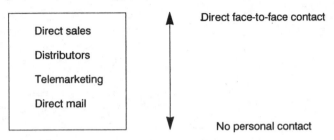

**Figure 4.1:** *Marketing channels*

Because it is an expensive channel to operate, direct sales is mainly restricted to high value industrial goods. Advertising expenditure is higher on consumer goods, particularly low value repeat-buy items such as food and household consumables. Consumer goods are usually sold through distributors, wholesalers and retailers rather than through direct selling. It is still normally necessary for the company to have a sales force to sell to these distributors, wholesalers and retailers.

Product characteristics will have a considerable influence on the mix of marketing channels that are finally selected. The number of levels of channels of distribution will also affect prices because of the level of discounts that will need to be built into the price structure.

### Direct sales

In a perfect world direct selling, with the salesperson and the customer, face to face would give a company the optimum

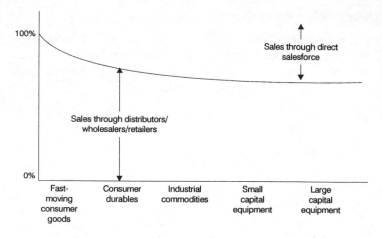

**Figure 4.2:** *The influence of product characteristics on distribution channels*

chance of getting the message across and closing the sale. In the real world this is just not cost-effective, and all companies employ a mixture of direct and indirect sales techniques.

The advantages of personal selling are:

- It allows two-way communication between the buyer and seller
- The salesperson can tailor the presentation to the individual needs of the customer
- The salesperson comes to know and be known by the customers
- The salesperson can negotiate directly on price, delivery and discounts
- The salesperson can close the sale
- The salesperson can monitor customer satisfaction levels.

## Distributors

In consumer goods industries, distributors could be retailers, wholesalers or even companies who sell to wholesalers. For industrial goods, it is not customary to use wholesale/retail outlets in the same way. Direct sales to customers make up a higher proportion of sales than with consumer goods, but the use of agents and distributors is widespread. A distributor takes over the selling role of the manufacturer and often has its own sales force to deal with customers.

A distributor would normally be expected to hold enough stock to service the geographical area for which he is responsible. Most distributors sell a range of products, so a product will not get the exclusive treatment through a distributor's sales force that it would through a company's own sales force.

A direct sales force can be structured:

- By product
- By area
- By account.

Distributors can be appointed on the same basis.

## Telemarketing

Telemarketing involves selling and marketing by telephone rather than by direct physical contact. It is most effective when it supplements the field sales force activity rather than completely replacing it. Whereas six to ten personal visits per day is normal for direct sales calls, 40 to 50 telephone calls can be made per day so telemarketing is very cost-effective.

The main advantages of telemarketing:

- More cost effective than direct sales force
- Frees up salesperson's time by reducing routine calling activity

- Increases frequency of customer contact
- Allows dormant accounts to be revived.

## Direct mail

Direct mail includes mail order business and mail shots. Mail shots involve sending information on a specific product by mail to potential customers on a mailing list. They rely for their success on the accuracy of the mailing list used, and a small return rate (typically 2 per cent) is considered quite normal.

## Physical distribution, warehousing and factory location

Physical distribution involves the holding of stock, communicating within the distribution network and the way the product is packaged for distribution. The proximity of the factory to its markets is more important with high bulk/low value goods than with sophisticated capital goods, but stocking at the factory, at warehouses or logistics centres is an important part of distribution strategy that will determine whether you can give as good a service as your competitors – or better.

## Customer service

At this stage, we are only interested in the aspects of customer service that affect distribution; in other words, the level of availability of the product to the customer. Distribution is about getting the product to the right place (for the customer) at the right time. Theoretically, you want to offer your customers 100 per cent availability. In practice this is not possible, because it is necessary to find a balance between the costs and benefits involved. The costs of extra availability cannot exceed the extra revenue that will be gained as a result.

In the distribution plan it is necessary to consider whether a change in marketing channels or physical distribution is necessary.

## The advertising and promotions plan

This plan comprises personnel, advertising and promotions.

### Personnel

Once you have selected your mix of distribution channels, you can decide on the personnel requirements of the plan. Your product will determine to some extent the channels that you use (see Figure 4.2 on page 34). In turn, the channels will determine to some extent the type of sales organisation that you need. A SWOT analysis for the sales organisation should indicate the weaknesses that need to be addressed and the opportunities that you can capitalise on.

You should detail your existing sales structure and, if there are changes, the proposed structure for the plan. Indicate which personnel are already in place and which are additional (or replacements!).

Figure 4.3 (overleaf) illustrates some of the changes in personnel required when a company restructures its sales force. In the original structure the UK sales manager is running the sales force and distribution. The direct sales force is selling to large key accounts, while the contracting companies and distributors are selling to end-users.

The existing structure lacks focus. In the new structure, the UK sales manager becomes the field sales manager. A sales engineer who has some expertise in the area becomes the product/sales manager for the water industry and a separate sales force is created to develop water industry sales. The general sales manager and distributor sales manager are new personnel who need to be recruited.

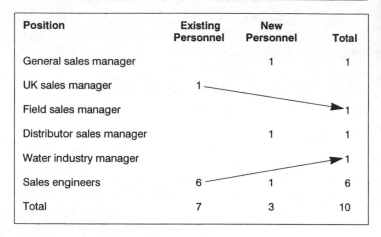

| Position | Existing Personnel | New Personnel | Total |
|---|---|---|---|
| General sales manager | | 1 | 1 |
| UK sales manager | 1 | | |
| Field sales manager | | | 1 |
| Distributor sales manager | | 1 | 1 |
| Water industry manager | | | 1 |
| Sales engineers | 6 | 1 | 6 |
| Total | 7 | 3 | 10 |

**Figure 4.3:** *New and existing sales personnel*

## Advertising and promotions

The purpose of advertising is to get a message across to the customer. Advertising operates at three levels – it *informs*, *persuades* and *reinforces*. Advertising to inform normally relates to the promotion of new products and services. Advertising to persuade is what most people understand as advertising. There is also the public relations side of advertising: promotional public relations, which includes media relations and exhibitions.

Because advertising on television and in the national press is very expensive, it mostly relates to consumer goods with large annual sales or services such as banking and insurance. The advertising of industrial and capital goods uses much narrower and more specific outlets, such as industry-specific magazines. In the same way, industrial products are normally on show at exhibitions specific to that industry, rather than at general trade fairs.

Figures 4.4 and 4.5 (overleaf) show examples of a press advertising schedule and exhibition cost schedule. The costs of these items will go into the advertising and promotions plan.

| Press advertising | | | | | | | | | | | | | | | | | | |
|---|---|---|---|---|---|---|---|---|---|---|---|---|---|---|---|---|---|---|
| Application water industry | | | | | | | | | Year: 19X6 | | | | | | | | | |
| Media | No. | Rate per insertion £ | Total cost £ | J | F | M | A | M | J | J | A | S | O | N | D | | | |
| Water & waste treatment | 4 | 900 | 3,600 | x | | | x | | | x | | | x | | | | | |
| Water services | 4 | 800 | 3,200 | | x | | | x | | | x | | | x | | | | |
| Water bulletin | 6 | 500 | 3,000 | x | | x | | x | | x | | x | | x | | | | |
| Water yearbook | 1 | 1,200 | 1,200 | x | | | | | | | | | | | | | | |
| Total cost | | | 11,000 | | | | | | | | | | | | | | | |

**Figure 4.4:** *Press advertising schedule*

## Costs and budgets

Strategies and action plans may be feasible, but are they cost-effective? If the cost of implementing the strategies and carrying out the action plans is greater than the contribution to company profits resulting from the additional sales forecast in the plan, you might as well forget the plan now – unless you can devise other strategies to achieve the same objectives.

How can you decide if your marketing plan is viable? Only by preparing a partial profit and loss account. For sales personnel, this can be the most difficult part of the whole process and it is wise to involve someone from

---

Exhibition costs

Name of exhibition: International Water
Location: NEC Birmingham
Date: 6th – 8th November 19x6

Stand size: 64m² (8m x 8m)
Stand contractor: Exhibition Contractors Ltd

*Costs*

|                                              | £      |
|----------------------------------------------|--------|
| Stand space rental                           | 8000   |
| Design, supply and build                     | 10,000 |
| Artwork, photographic panels                 | 5000   |
| Rental of carpets, furniture, lights, phone, etc | 3000   |
| Hotel bills/expenditure for stand staff      | 2000   |
| Totals                                       | 28,000 |

**Figure 4.5:** *Schedule of expenditure for a major exhibition*

your finance and accounting department to help you to prepare the partial profit and loss account you need for your plan.

## Profit and loss account

The profit and loss account is a summary of the success or failure of the transactions of a company over a period of time. It lists income generated and costs incurred. From the point of view of a marketing plan, we are not interested in anything below the line of operating profit, because marketing activities will only affect items reported above this line in the profit and loss account. An example of a profit and loss account down to the operating profit level is shown in Figure 4.6.

It is important to understand the key items reported in the profit and loss account.

|  |  |  | £000 |
|---|---|---|---|
|  | Turnover |  | 6000 |
| less | Cost of sales |  | 4000 |
|  | Gross profit |  | 2000 |
| less | Distribution costs | 100 |  |
|  | Operating expenses | 850 |  |
|  |  |  | 950 |
|  | Operating profit |  | 1050 |

**Figure 4.6:** *An example of a profit and loss account*

## Turnover

The turnover is the total amount of revenue earned during the year from the company's normal trading operations.

## Cost of sales

This represents the direct cost of making the product. The costs are primarily labour and materials.

## Gross profit

When the cost of sales is removed from the turnover, the resulting figure is the gross profit. This gives a direct comparison between what the product can be sold for and what it costs to make. This 'margin' has to be sufficient to cover all the costs and overheads incurred in running the business.

## Other costs

These would include distribution costs, administration and operating expenses such as the cost of running the sales and marketing department, together with advertising and promotional costs. It would also include head office

41

salaries, rates, electricity, depreciation and the cost of research and development.

## Operating profit

This is the key figure in the accounts as far as we are concerned. It is the net result of trading for the year when total sales revenue is compared with the expenses incurred in earning that revenue. It is the ultimate measure of whether it has been worthwhile staying in business.

Before you start budgeting for your marketing plan you need to familiarise yourself with the accounting practices used in your own company or business unit. Obtain copies of your company's profit and loss account and get your accounts department to explain how the distribution costs and operating expenses are calculated and allocated.

## Budgeting for the cost of a marketing plan

A marketing plan is part of the company business plan. Individual marketing plans are ultimately collated into the overall company marketing plan. The principles are the same whether you are preparing the sales budget for the overall company marketing plan or calculating the effect of an individual plan. However, in budgeting and evaluating individual plans, you need only consider part of the company budgeting process. This is shown in Figure 4.7.

Only if your product is new or you anticipate considerable increases in business from your plan may major capital investment also be required. Obviously, if your plan includes an increase in field sales personnel, you will need to budget for more company cars and laptop computers.

With a marketing plan for an individual product or market, we are considering only the additional turnover generated by the plan and the costs associated with its implementation, not the total company turnover and costs.

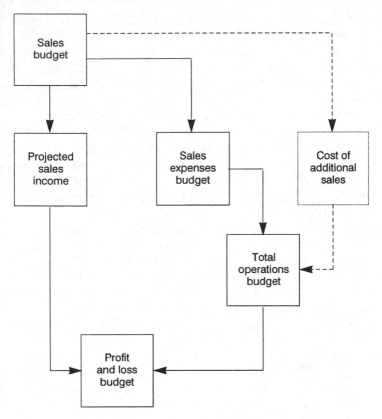

**Figure 4.7:** *Budgeting for additional sales*

A number of techniques will allow you to predict whether the extra business that you generate from your plan will be profitable or not. One of the simplest is to cost up all the expenses that you intend to occur in implementing your plan and compare these with the contribution that will be generated by the additional sales turnover resulting from your plan. Include the costs of all the actions plans for all the strategies you intend to use. For individual plans this method is quite adequate and we will use it here. (When a new product is being introduced, more complex techniques such as break-even analysis or payback analysis can also be used. These techniques are explained further in *The Marketing Plan*, also published by Kogan Page.)

In preparing a profit and loss account budget, we start at the top with the forecast sales. Here we show only the *additional sales*. The cost of sales is the direct cost, in materials and labour, of making the budgeted amount of product sold. The gross profit includes the margin needed to cover other costs and to contribute to profits.

Most of the costs incurred in carrying out a marketing plan will relate to the sales and marketing department, but you should also consider administrative recharges for the management of company cars, allocation of office space (rent/rates/heating/lighting), and computer management and maintenance, which will involve other departments.

The costs incurred by the sales and marketing department represent the costs of extra items such as literature, advertising and exhibitions as well as the cost of salaries and travelling expenses related to the additional staff included in the plan. The costs of the existing sales force will already be included in the overall company profit and loss budget and do not therefore need to be included again.

A partial profit and loss account for additional sales is shown in Figure 4.8.

The plan shows a loss in its first year and only breaks even in year two. This is quite normal. It is often necessary to invest first and reap the rewards later. However, if break even was later than the second year it would be wise to reconsider the plan.

|                                          | 19X6<br>£k | 19X7<br>£k | 19X8<br>£k |
|------------------------------------------|------------|------------|------------|
| Invoiced sales                           | 260.0      | 576.0      | 937.0      |
| Cost of sales                            | 158.6      | 339.8      | 534.1      |
| Gross profit                             | 101.4      | 236.2      | 402.9      |
| *Sales & marketing costs*                |            |            |            |
| Salaries                                 | 75.0       | 78.0       | 81.1       |
| Recruitment                              | 6.0        |            |            |
| Travel/ent                               | 7.0        | 7.6        | 7.9        |
| Car costs                                | 6.0        | 6.2        | 6.5        |
| Advertising                              | 11.0       | 11.5       | 12.0       |
| Exhibitions                              | 28.0       |            | 15.0       |
| Literature                               | 5.0        | 25.0       | 20.0       |
| Sundry items                             |            | 5.0        | 6.0        |
| Total sales costs                        | 138.0      | 133.3      | 148.5      |
| Administration costs                     | 20.0       | 20.8       | 21.6       |
| Data processing costs                    | 5.0        | 5.5        | 6.0        |
| Distribution costs                       | 6.9        | 7.2        | 7.5        |
| Total operating expenses<br>(Relating to plan) | 169.9  | 166.8      | 183.6      |
| Operating profit<br>(Relating to plan)   | (68.5)     | 69.4       | 219.3      |

**Figure 4.8:** *The effect on the profit and loss account of the additional operating expenses for implementing a marketing plan*

# 5

# WRITING THE PLAN

The written plan should be clear and concise, and excessive or irrelevant detail excluded. The bulk of the internal and external market research information collected during the preparation process should not be included in the written plan, since this would only confuse the reader. Detail of all the individual action plans should also be excluded from the main document, although a summary of very important action plans may be included. Other key information that you want to include should be put in appendices, not in the main document. Your priority should be to make the plan easy to read.

The following points give some guidelines for the written plan:

- Start each complete section on a new page, even if this means that some pages have only five or ten lines of text on them

- When listing key points, use double spacing

- Do not try to cram too many figures on to one page

- Do not reduce the size of documents used in the plan so much that they become difficult to read
- Use a reasonable font size when printing the document
- If the plan is too long it will not be read, so be ruthless and cut out unnecessary text
- Do not use jargon that may not be understood by all those who will receive the plan, and be sure to explain any abbreviations the first time they appear.

If you write the plan carefully, you can use many of the individual sections as presentation slides.

## Contents list

You should start with a table of contents so the reader can quickly locate the various sections of the plan. Figure 5.1 (overleaf) shows how the table of contents should be set out. Depending on the scope of your plan, you may need to omit or combine certain sections.

## Introduction

This gives the background to the plan, the reasons for its preparation, and outlines its purposes and uses. For example, a company selling a product to the water industry could write the following introduction to its plan:

'UK sales have stagnated in recent years. The company has always sold a reasonable amount of product to the water industry, but it has never been a key activity area. Because of this, we knew little of the industry or of the potential in it for our product. With the enforcement of EU directives for water treatment and sewage disposal, the industry is carrying out a major capital improvement programme. It was therefore felt by the sales and marketing director that we needed to analyse our position in the market and prepare for growth to take advantage of the increased level of spending by the industry.'

*Contents*



**Figure 5.1:** *Contents list of a complete marketing plan*

## Executive summary

The summary should present the key points of the plan in a clear and concise form. It should not be too long or verbose. Anyone reading the plan should be able to understand the essence of the plan from this summary, which should always include:

- The underlying assumptions on which the plan is based
- The objectives of the plan
- The time-scale over which the plan will be implemented.

Although you can draft an executive summary at any time, you cannot finalise the text until the plan is complete.

An example of an executive summary for a UK marketing plan is given below.

'Although our total sales in the UK market have fallen, sales of filters have tripled in the last three years. The increase in filter sales has been mainly into the water industry. Our problem area has been ball valves, where we only have a 10 per cent market share, with low sales to the water industry. We currently have market shares in the water industry of 10 per cent for filters and 5 per cent for valves. We believe that if economic conditions remain stable, we will be able to gain market share in this expanding market. Also, the packaging of our filters and valves together will give us a competitive advantage.

The objective of this plan is to achieve 10 per cent growth in UK sales in real terms over the next three years, doubling our water industry market share for filters to 20 per cent and for ball valves to 10 per cent of the projected market in 19X8. In doing so, we intend to increase UK overall gross margins from 39 to 43 per cent by 19X8. This plan details how this can be

> achieved with an investment in personnel and resources, but without any major additional investment in plant and machinery.'

# Situation analysis

In the written plan, the situation analysis should include only the summaries of the external and internal marketing research and the key resulting SWOT analysis. These are included under the headings:

- The assumptions
- A summary of historical and budgeted sales
- A review of strategic markets
- A review of key products
- A review of key sales areas.

There will be some overlap between the reviews of strategic markets, key products and key sales areas, because it is possible to show the mix in different ways. The important thing is to present the information in a way that highlights the key points you are trying to convey. Often, the SWOT analyses are put together in the appendix.

## Assumptions

These are the key facts and assumptions on which the plan is based. They should be few in number and relate only to key issues which would significantly affect the success of the plan's marketing objectives.

Each assumption should be a brief factual statement. For example:

- The £/$ exchange rate will remain in the range $1.5–$1.7: £1 for the next 12 months

- Interest rates will not increase by more than 1 per cent over the next three years
- The present import restraint level of 10 per cent of the market share is respected by the Japanese.

## Sales

In this section you should include historical sales going back three years, together with sales forecasts for the next three years. Unless you state otherwise, it will be assumed that the years shown in your forecast are calendar years. Use invoiced sales rather than order intake figures as the basis of the plan, because other departments in the company, such as production and finance, can only operate on sales figures. You will, however, need to include order intake figures in your plan as well, because these will be the order budgets that the sales department will work to. More detail would normally be included with regard to the next 12 months' sales forecast, since this will become the annual budget for the product or area covered by the plan.

You would normally only include the sales projection for the entire area and related products. A more detailed breakdown into individual products and sub-areas would be included under key products, key sales areas or in the appendix to the plan. The format for setting out this information follows the guidelines given in Chapter 2. An example is shown in Figure 5.2 (overleaf).

## Strategic markets

In this section you should include historical information and forecasts for the company's sales in key industry sectors, which can be presented in two ways: by (i) showing the percentage of company sales into each market; or (ii)

| The Equipment Manufacturing Company Sales figures (historical and forecast) | | | | | |
|---|---|---|---|---|---|
| Sales area: UK | | | ◄——forecast——► | | |
| Year | 19X3 | 19X4 | 19X5 | 19X6 | 19X7 | 19X8 |
| Filters | 200 | 450 | 600 | 750 | 900 | 1050 |
| Valves | 1400 | 1200 | 1000 | 1060 | 1151 | 1287 |
| Components | 300 | 350 | 400 | 450 | 525 | 600 |
| Total | 1900 | 2000 | 2000 | 2260 | 2576 | 2937 |

**Figure 5.2:** *Sales projection for UK (all values in £k)*

by showing the percentage share of individual markets that the company believes it has.

Only include your key markets; ideally, this should be between three and six industries, because if you limit yourself to one, you will be very vulnerable to changes or fluctuations within that industry.

This type of information can be presented either in tabular or graphic form. Figure 5.3 shows an example in graphic form.

It would be helpful to include some background notes on the key industries.

## Key products

This section lists your key products and details technological and commercial factors relating to them. This would include the results of the SWOT analysis on your products and those of your competitors. The information could be presented in a similar format to the data on strategic markets, or it could be included in a product portfolio matrix. An example of a product portfolio matrix was shown in Figure 3.3.

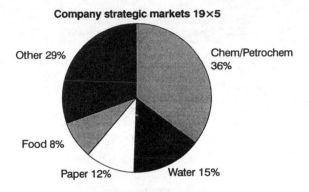

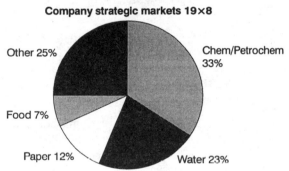

**Figure 5.3:** *Graphic representation of strategic markets*

## Key sales areas

This information is presented in the same way as that on strategic markets, but is given in relation to geographical areas rather than industry sectors. The information can be presented in tabular or graphic form.

In the narrative of your plan you should include relevant information on the size of each key market, growth rates, your position in each market now and your projected

| The Equipment Manufacturing Company Sales figures (historical and forecast) Sales area: UK Product: Ball valves | | | | forecast | |
|---|---|---|---|---|---|
| Year | 19X3 | 19X4 | 19X5 | 19X6 | 19X7 | 19X8 |
| South | 295 | 250 | 230 | 240 | 250 | 260 |
| Midlands | 485 | 415 | 360 | 370 | 390 | 420 |
| North | 525 | 420 | 300 | 325 | 351 | 422 |
| Wales | 45 | 55 | 60 | 65 | 70 | 75 |
| Scotland/NI | 50 | 60 | 50 | 70 | 90 | 110 |
| Total UK | 1400 | 1200 | 1000 | 1070 | 1151 | 1287 |

**Figure 5.4:** *Representation of key sales areas*

future position, as well as comments which may relate to your distributor, agent or other methods of distribution.

## Marketing objectives

This is a list of the objectives to be achieved, quantified in terms of order intake, sales turnover, market share and profit. In the written plan list your key objectives only.

Examples of a company's objectives for its UK plan are given below:

- To increase UK sales by 10 per cent per year in real terms for the next three years
- To double ball valve sales to the water industry within three years
- To increase sales of packages to 50 units within three years
- To double market share for filters in the water industry by 19X8
- To double distributor sales in Scotland and NI by 19X8
- To increase overall gross margins from 39 to 43 per cent by 19X8

# Marketing strategies

Indicate whether you are adopting defensive, developing or attacking strategies – or a mixture of different types. The individual strategies should then be divided up under the headings of the four main elements of the marketing mix:

- Strategies relating to products
- Strategies relating to pricing
- Strategies relating to advertising/promotion
- Strategies relating to distribution.

There may be some overlap between the individual categories, but this does not matter so long as all of the strategies are listed. The example below includes a mixture of *developing* and *attacking* strategies.

## Products

- Package products (ball valves with filters)
- Design new ball valve
- Design replacement for Type S filter

## Pricing

- Discount policy for Type S filters will be progressively withdrawn
- Penetration policy will be adopted with packages as this will help us to sell more valves
- Penetration policy will be adopted on Type K filters since these generate a large proportion of replacement cartridges

## Promotion

- Change sales force organisation
- Restructure sales management
- Increase advertising

- Use mail shots
- Increase exhibition coverage

*Distribution*
- Change distribution
- Increase own sales coverage

## Schedule of what, where and how

This is the master schedule showing the programme for the implementation of the action plans. Each action plan should be listed either in the master schedule or in a sub-schedule for the functions of product, pricing, promotion or distribution. These schedules indicate to each department and to each member of staff their responsibilities and the timetable for carrying them out. They should take the form of bar charts. An example of a master schedule is shown in Figure 5.5.

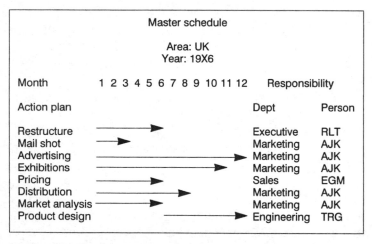

**Figure 5.5:** *Example of a master schedule*

Detailed action plans should not be included in the main body of the marketing plan, but could be included in an appendix.

## Sales promotion

Under this heading you should detail your advertising and promotions plan. This includes your personnel requirements as well as the costs of advertising and sales promotion.

Define the mix of distribution channels that you will be using and the structure of your sales organisation, including any changes that you intend to make as part of your plan. Include a list of existing and additional sales personnel as well as an organisation chart for the sales department. The charts can be in an appendix to the main plan.

Include the details and costs of your advertising and sales promotion campaigns. A detailed advertising and promotions schedule for the next 12 months should be in an appendix.

## Budgets and the profit and loss account

The total cost of implementing the plan is the minimum information that needs to be included. It should confirm that the return in increased contribution and profit justifies the expenditure in the action plans and the advertising and promotion plan. The budgeted extra costs will have an effect on the company profit and loss account. The additional sales projected by the plan and the extra costs involved must be presented in the written plan in a way that shows the extra contribution that the plan will make to company profits. The figures should be presented as shown in Figure 4.8. They can also be presented as a complete profit and loss account for the area and products of the plan: see the example shown in Figure 5.6 (overleaf).

|                        | 19X6 £k | 19X7 £k | 19X8 £k |
|------------------------|---------|---------|---------|
| Invoiced sales         | 2260    | 2576    | 2937    |
| Cost of sales          | 1356    | 1507    | 1674    |
| Gross profit           | 904     | 1069    | 1263    |
| *Sales & marketing costs* |      |         |         |
| Salaries               | 239.8   | 249.4   | 259.4   |
| Recruitment            | 9.1     | 3.2     | 3.4     |
| Travel/entertaining    | 37.9    | 39.4    | 41.0    |
| Car costs              | 20.4    | 21.2    | 22.0    |
| Advertising            | 21.3    | 22.2    | 23.0    |
| Exhibitions            | 38.3    | 11.0    | 26.4    |
| Literature             | 15.3    | 36.0    | 31.7    |
| Sundry items           | 10.3    | 10.7    | 11.1    |
| Total sales costs      | 392.4   | 393.1   | 418.0   |
| Administration costs   | 159.0   | 166.4   | 174.1   |
| Data processing costs  | 32.0    | 33.3    | 34.6    |
| Distribution costs     | 60.0    | 65.0    | 70.0    |
| Total operating expenses | 643.4 | 657.8   | 696.7   |
| Operating profit       | 260.6   | 411.2   | 566.3   |

**Figure 5.6:** *Example of a profit and loss account.*

## Controls and update procedures

It is important to have a suitable monitoring and control system to measure performance in achieving the objectives of the marketing plan and to recommend corrective action where necessary. This monitoring and control system should be included in the written plan.

The control process involves:

■ Establishing standards: these should take into account budgeted sales and costs and the time-scales for the implementation of the action plans

- Measuring performance: this means comparing actual performance against the standards

- Proposing measures to correct deviations from the standard and detailing corrective procedures to be implemented if the variation from standard exceeds certain limits. These limits should be defined in the written plan.

The control system will affect the people who are responsible for implementing the plan rather than the schedules and costs themselves. It should be easy to operate and allow reasonable variations from the standards before coming into action.

A marketing plan is not set in stone. As you implement it you will find that economic conditions may change, certain strategies may not be as effective as you thought and there may be delays in the implementation of some action plans. Because of this, an update procedure should be included in the written plan. This may simply state 'This plan is to be revised every 12 months'. Certainly, all marketing plans should be updated on an annual basis.

# 6

# PRESENTING THE PLAN, FOLLOW UP AND REVISION

Once the plan is complete, it must be communicated to those who must agree to its implementation and to those who will actually implement it.

A marketing plan is a sensitive and confidential document that would be of considerable interest to competitors. Personnel do move on and take information with them. Copies should therefore only be given to personnel who really need them, to senior executives and to the heads of departments.

## Presenting the plan

Presentation of the plan needs to be even more clear and concise than the written document itself. You may only have an hour – or even less – to present a plan that has taken many months to prepare.

Nowadays, everyone uses overhead presentations, but some types of presentation package make a greater impact than others. I favour the use of the Microsoft Office software package with the Powerpoint presentation programme. Powerpoint is *extremely powerful* and, if used properly, can make a tremendous impression. The slides are prepared on a PC and the presentation can then be made from the PC or the slides printed off on to overhead transparencies. The package itself is in colour – so *use it!* If you prepare the presentation on overhead transparencies they can be printed in colour. Powerpoint really comes into its own if you make the presentation from a PC, and this can be done in a number of ways:

- You can use a PC with a reasonably large screen
- You can connect a laptop to a larger PC screen
- You can use an 'overlay' projector on top of an overhead projector. (This requires a powerful overhead projector with a strong light)
- You can also use a special 'projector' which can be connected to a PC.

You should use large font sizes on your slides, use a large screen and make the presentation in a room that can be properly darkened to ensure that everyone can see the presentation and read all the slides. Your presentation will look more professional if you prepare a template with your company name and logo on it.

By using Powerpoint you can prepare slides from scratch, or import files from Word or Excel. These can be text, tables or graphics. Powerpoint also includes a full range of graphic images called 'Clipart', such as maps of countries and continents, images of computers, and even little cartoon people. The use of some of these items in the right places will brighten up any presentation. But do not overdo it! Other techniques that can be used include bringing in bullet points one by one on a slide to avoid your audience trying to read the whole slide at once instead of listening to your presentation.

Some examples of presentation slides are shown in Figures 6.1, 6.2 and 6.3.

---

**Marketing plan 19 × 6**

### KEY OBJECTIVES

- Increase UK sales by 10% per year

- Double ball valve sales to water industry

- Increase package sales to 50 per year

- Double filter market share in water industry

- Double distributor sales in Scotland/NI

- Increase gross margins from 39 to 43%

**EMC Ltd**

---

**Figure 6.1:** *Objectives*

## Follow-up and revision

After presentation, the plan must be implemented. The schedules and action plans will be followed and the results become apparent. The control and update procedures will allow progress to be monitored and any necessary changes to be made.

Most companies use their marketing plans as a basis for the annual budgeting process. And so the iterative process

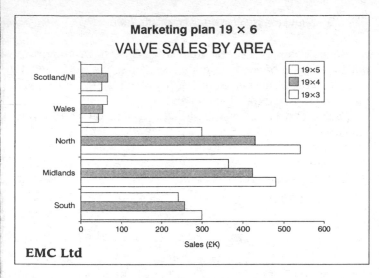

**Figure 6.2:** *Valve sales by area*

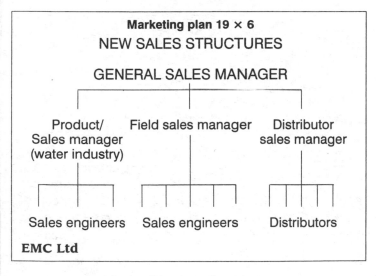

**Figure 6.3:** *New sales structure*

continues: from marketing plan to budget, from budget to update/revision of marketing plan, and on to the next budget. This procedure can be simplified if you set up basic formats for both your marketing plans and budgets on your PC. The plan itself can be set up as a blank format on Word, with blank spreadsheets in Excel. If you lay it out with numbered pages, you can impose the discipline on your colleagues so that a common company standard is used for marketing plans, budgets and their presentation. This will also make it easier for those with less training or experience in marketing planning than you to prepare the plans that are necessary for their part of the business.

The biggest advantage of a common format is that any individual plan can easily be incorporated into the overall company marketing plan, and sets of figures can be added together in interlinked spreadsheets.

## Conclusion

This book is a quick guide to marketing planning. If you follow the procedures shown, it will make your company's marketing planning easier and more professional in the future. Practice makes better, but not perfect, and each time the marketing planning process is followed through, the results will improve.

With the best planning in the world, markets are still affected by forces outside your control: but with a proper marketing plan and an understanding of the marketing planning process, you can adapt to the changing conditions of the competitive world in which we live.